Dear Janelle & Tyrel

We are so proud of all you have achieved.
We know that sometimes it is not easy
but you never gave up. You continue to
believe in THRIVE and be a big part of
our team. You have been on your first PB
Live workshop and we couldn't be more
proud. We are so excited for your fitness
journey and all the people you are going
to help.

Thank you for coming to convention.
We love you and are grateful for your friend-
ship.

Bella, Kris & Jayden

on to last page ☺   July 19, 2018

I
believe
in
you

First Edition
20 19 18 17 16   5 4 3 2 1

Text © 2016 Gibbs Smith
Illustrations © 2016 Gibbs Smith

Published by
Gibbs Smith
P.O. Box 667
Layton, Utah 84041

1.800.835.4993 orders
www.gibbs-smith.com

Designed by Sky Hatter

Printed and bound in Hong Kong

Gibbs Smith books are printed on either recycled, 100% post-consumer waste, FSC-certified papers or on paper produced from sustainable PEFC-certified forest/controlled wood source. Learn more at www.pefc.org.

Library of Congress Cataloging-in-Publication Data
Library of Congress Control Number: 2016930183
ISBN: 9781423644804

I believe in you

Illustrated by Sky Hatter

GIBBS SMITH
TO ENRICH AND INSPIRE HUMANKIND

Chapter 1

She believed she could,

so she did.

—R.S. Grey

It looks
good on you.

Be somebody's

sunshine today.

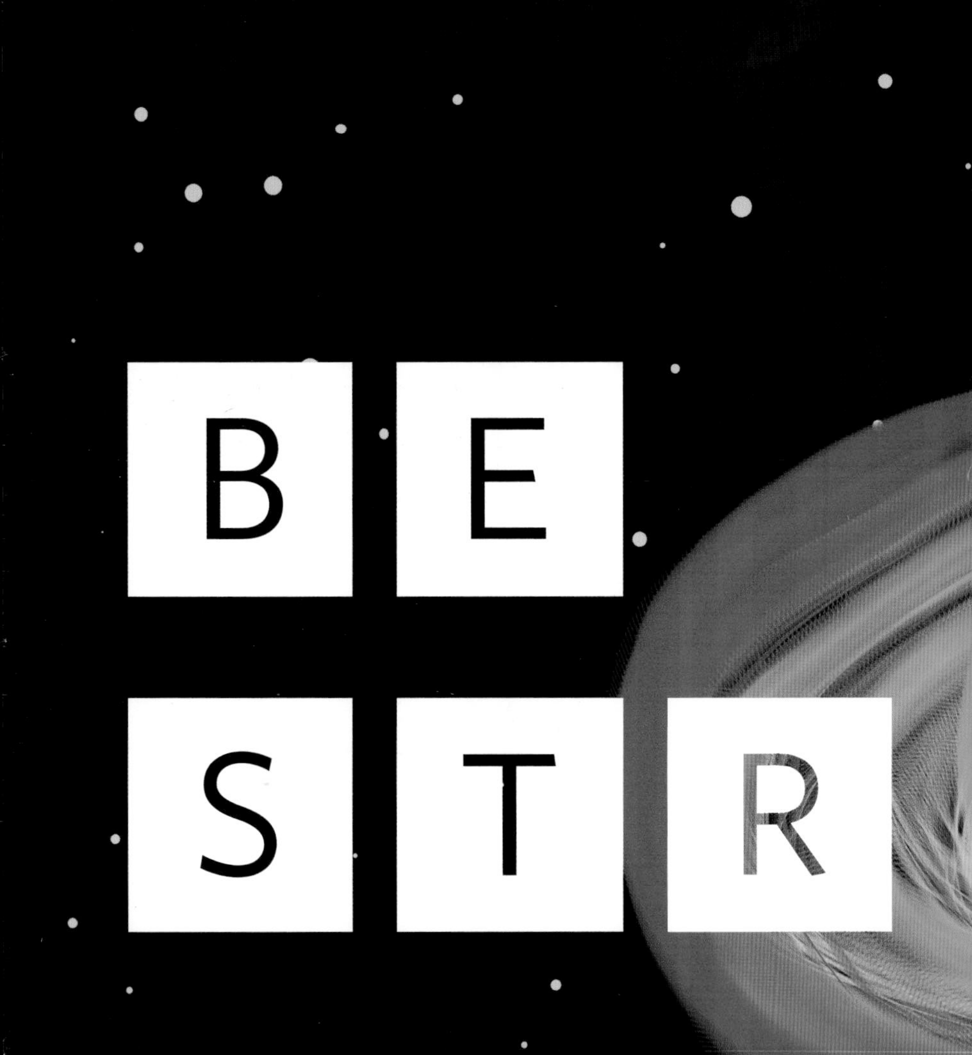
B E
S T R

IT'S
OK

to
not
be
OK.

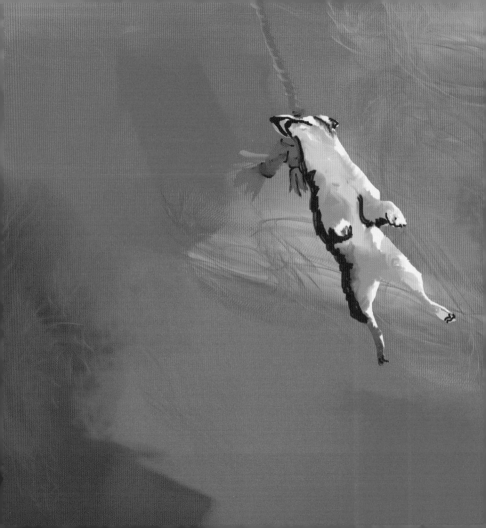

When you

come to the end of your

rope,

tie a knot and hang on.

NEVER COMPARE YOUR BEGINNING

TO SOMEONE ELSE'S MIDDLE.

—Jon Acuff

I AM YOUR BIGGEST FAN.

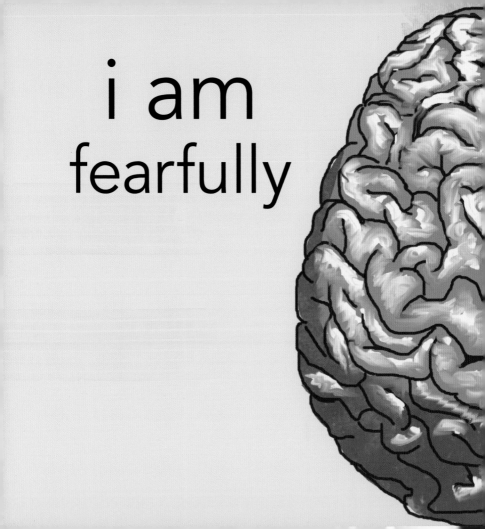

and WONDERFULLY MADE

THINK GOOD THOUGHTS

GOOD THINGS
are going to
happen today.

Make some lemonade.

We cannot direct the wind,
but we can adjust the sails.

— Thomas S. Monson

I believe in you.

NG

IN THERE

Always be yourself.*

*Unless you can be a unicorn, then always be a unicorn.

YOU NEED

DEEP IN

BEFORE

YOUR

TO BE BURIED

THE DIRT

YOU CAN FIND

BLOOM.

—ROZ INGA

CHASE YOUR DREAMS

LIFE IS BETTER
with friends.

IT'S NOT WHETHER YOU GET KNOCKED DOWN,

IT'S WHETHER
YOU GET UP.
—Vince Lombardi

Reach as high as you can,
and then reach a little higher.

There you will find magic
and possibility. And maybe
even cookies.

—Marc Johns

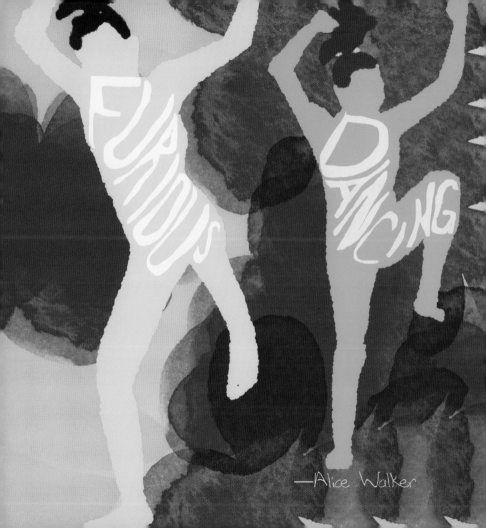

FURIOUS DANCING

—Alice Walker

SUCCESS

comes in

CANS

not can'ts

Just when the caterpillar thought the world was over,

it became a
butterfly.

WHEN IT IS DARK ENOUGH,

YOU CAN SEE STARS.

—*Ralph Waldo Emerson*

A woman is like a tea bag.

You never know
how strong she is
until you put her
in hot water.

Life is like riding

To keep your

balance,

you must keep

a bicycle.

oving.

—Albert Einstein

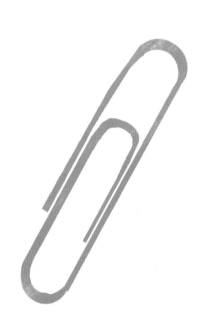

Do what you **CAN,** with what you've **GOT, WHERE** you are.

–Squire Bill Widener

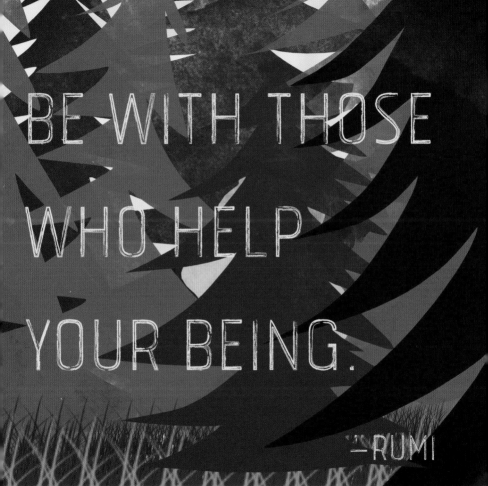

THE TRUTH WILL SET YOU FREE,

but first
it will piss
you off.

—*Gloria Steinem*

POUR YOURSELF A

drink,

PUT ON SOME

lipstick,

AND PULL YOURSELF

together.

—ELIZABETH TAYLOR

Keep on

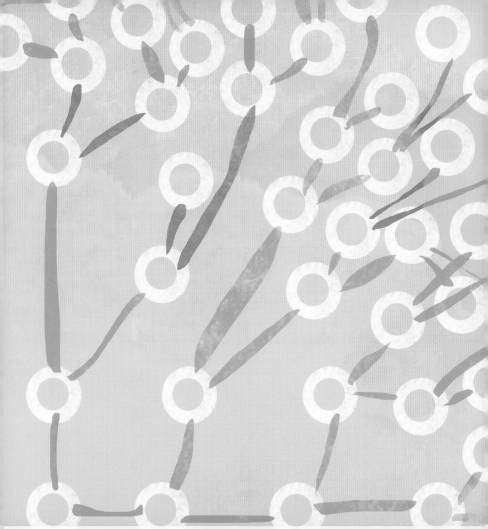

Let your soul stand cool and composed before a million universes.

–Walt Whitman

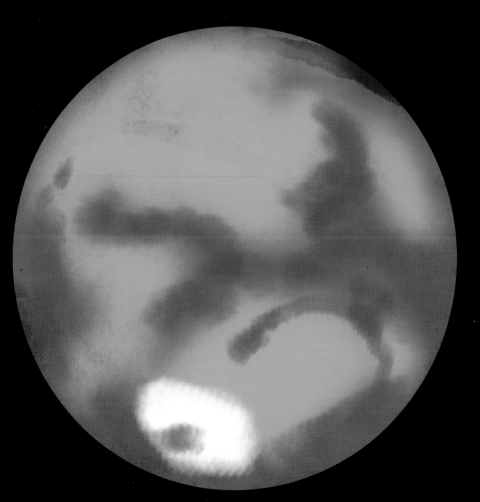

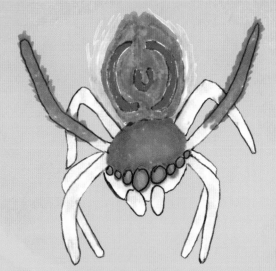

The things that make you

DIFFERENT

are the things that

MAKE YOU